COLOGNE/DUSSELDORF

COLOGNE AT A GLANCE

Wallraf-Richartz-Museum
Oswald Mathias Ungers' celebrated building
holds one of Germany's great art collections,
including much from the Cologne School.
See p070

Gross St Martin
This Rhineside Romanesque church was built
between 1150 and 1240 and restored in 1985.
Gross St Martin 9

Kölner Opernhaus
Wilhelm Riphahn's 1957 truncated modernist
pyramid is one of the city's architectural
highlights and boasts a gorgeous interior.
See p074

Ludwig Museum
This distinctive zinc-clad serrated-roofed shed
harbours a vast display of contemporary art.
Heinrich-Böll-Platz, T 0221 26 165

Kölner Dom
The centuries-old symbol of Cologne can
be spied from almost any point in the city.
See p014

Colonius
Spiking the sky like a concrete needle, the
1981 telecoms tower reached 266m in 2004
after a radio antenna was added by helicopter.
See p009

Hohenzollernbrücke
Opened in 1911, this 410m railway bridge was
designed by Franz Heinrich Schwechten and
is one of the most heavily used in Germany.

Köln Turm
Jean Nouvel's shimmering glass tower is
a bold statement of Cologne's ambition.
See p010

INTRODUCTION
THE CHANGING FACE OF THE URBAN SCENE

Germany's fourth-largest city traditionally attracted visitors with its Romanesque churches, medieval history and brewhouses, but now Cologne also offers world-class contemporary art, design and fashion, and has a palpable bustle that is at odds with its laidback reputation. Its early 1990s heyday waned when Reunification lured labels, artists and events such as Popkomm to Berlin, but Cologne's creative tradition has always been strong (favourite sons include architect Gottfried Böhm, Nobel Prize-winning author Heinrich Böll and electronic music pioneer Karlheinz Stockhausen) and the city has bounced back. Today, it balances major events such as Art Cologne and KölnDesign with an independent scene centred on the Belgian Quarter, where the streets brim with boutiques and cutting-edge galleries (there are more than 100 across the city).

A 25-minute ride to the north is Dusseldorf, Cologne's smaller, wealthier and, let's be honest, prettier sibling. The capital of the North Rhine-Westphalia region lacks the urban punch of its rival but offers much in the way of culture – Paul Klee, Joseph Beuys and Gerhard Richter hail from the Dusseldorf School – while the swish Media Harbour, with its buildings by Frank Gehry, Steven Holl and David Chipperfield, represents the contemporary city. The surrounding countryside was once the engine room of the German economic miracle. In a sign of how much has changed here, the coal mines are now cultural centres and the slag heaps are ski slopes.

ESSENTIAL INFO

FACTS, FIGURES AND USEFUL ADDRESSES

TOURIST OFFICES
Kardinal-Höffner-Platz 1, Cologne
T 0221 2213 0400
www.cologne-tourism.com
Immermannstrasse 65b, Dusseldorf
T 0211 1720 2844
www.duesseldorf-tourismus.de

TRANSPORT
Car hire
Avis (Cologne)
T 0221 913 0062
Hertz (Dusseldorf)
T 0211 357 025
Taxis
Taxi-Ruf (Cologne)
T 0221 2882
Taxi Dusseldorf
T 0211 33 333
Trains
InterCity Express
www.bahn.de
Trains run regularly between Cologne and
Dusseldorf, taking around 25 minutes

EMERGENCY SERVICES
Fire and ambulance
T 112
Police
T 110
24-hour pharmacy
www.aponet.de (For the full list)

CONSULATES
British Consulate
Yorckstrasse 19, Dusseldorf
T 0211 94 480
www.ukingermany.fco.gov.uk
US Consulate
Willi-Becker-Allee 10, Dusseldorf
T 0211 788 8927
duesseldorf.usconsulate.gov

POSTAL SERVICES
Post office
Trankgasse 1, Cologne
T 01 802 3333
Shipping
Mail Boxes Etc
Dillenburger Strasse 27, Cologne
T 0221 261 1811

BOOKS
Billiards at Half-Past Nine
by Heinrich Böll (Penguin Classics)
**Gerhard Richter, Zufall, The Cologne
Cathedral Window and 4,900 Colours**
by Stephan Diederichs, Birgit Pelzer and
Barbara Schock-Werner (Verlag der
Buchhandlung Walther Konig)

WEBSITES
Art/culture
www.museenkoeln.de
Newspaper
www.spiegel.de/international

EVENTS
Art Cologne
www.artcologne.com
Cologne Carnival
www.koelnerkarneval1.de

COST OF LIVING
**Taxi from Cologne/Bonn Airport
to city centre**
€35
Cappuccino
€2.80
Packet of cigarettes
€4.90
Daily newspaper
€1.20
Bottle of champagne
€35

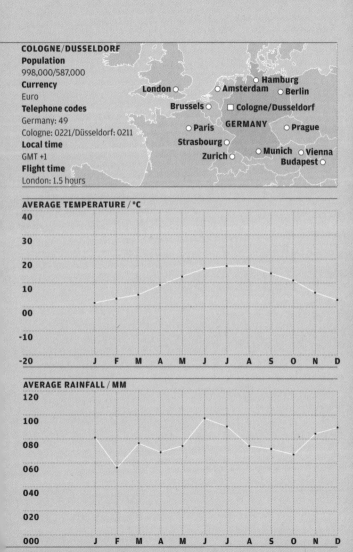

COLOGNE/DUSSELDORF
Population
998,000/587,000
Currency
Euro
Telephone codes
Germany: 49
Cologne: 0221/Düsseldorf: 0211
Local time
GMT +1
Flight time
London: 1.5 hours

Hamburg
London ○   ○ Amsterdam   ○ Berlin
Brussels ○   □ Cologne/Dusseldorf
○ Paris   GERMANY   ○ Prague
Strasbourg ○
Zurich ○   ○ Munich ○ Vienna
Budapest ○

AVERAGE TEMPERATURE / °C

40
30
20
10
00
-10
-20
    J F M A M J J A S O N D

AVERAGE RAINFALL / MM

120
100
080
060
040
020
000
    J F M A M J J A S O N D

NEIGHBOURHOODS

THE AREAS YOU NEED TO KNOW AND WHY

To help you navigate the city, we've chosen the most interesting districts (see below and the map inside the back cover) and colour-coded our featured venues, according to their location; those venues that are outside these areas are not coloured.

EHRENFELD

This up-and-coming working-class quarter is still a bit rough around the edges along main drag Venloer Strasse, but the side streets, especially Körnerstrasse, host funky boutiques, such as product design store Utensil (see p081), interesting bars, and plenty of hip cafés and nightlife.

NEUSTADT NORD

Centred around 1960s-era Ebertplatz, Nordstadt has a low-key, neighbourhood charm. Cologne's commercialism thins out here, and is superseded by local hangouts such as King Georg (see p048) and Elektra (see p050) and some of the city's best cinemas, including the arty Filmhaus (Maybach Strasse 111, T 0221 2227 1020).

SÜDSTADT

Quiet and unassuming for most of the year, Südstadt is transformed during the week-long Kölner Karneval, which kicks off on the Thursday before Lent. The area is home to the pretty Volksgarten park and the Rheinauhafen harbour development, signalled by the Kranhäuser (see p015).

KWARTIER LATÄNG

Cologne's student quarter is predictably lively and a little grungy. However, there are a number of more stylish spots, such as Feynsinn Café (see p052) on the lovely Rathenauplatz, and the funk- and soul-soundtracked hangout Boogaloo Bar (Roonstrasse 52, T 0177 784 4858).

DUSSELDORF

The Altstadt in Dusseldorf has been dubbed 'the longest bar in the world' with 300 drinking holes squeezed into half a square kilometre. It largely escaped the Allied air raids during the war and has an elegant spread of historic buildings – a highlight is the Basilica St Lambertus (Stiftsplatz 7).

BELGISCHES VIERTEL

The beating heart of cool Cologne, the Belgian Quarter stretches from busy Rudolfplatz to hip Aachener Strasse. A microcosm of the city, it's relaxed yet buzzy, packed with eateries, swanky bars, including Ivory Lounge (see p048), and boutiques like Chiang 13 (see p080). The streets throng with a fashionable crowd.

DEUTZ

Across the Hohenzollernbrücke on the east bank of the Rhine, businessy Deutz is a hub of congress and exhibition centres and corporate HQs. What it lacks in a happening scene, it makes up for with its Rhine promenade, beer gardens and killer city views back over the water to the city.

ALTSTADT

Cologne's Old Town is a labyrinth of streets that give up no end of treasures. There are landmarks like the world-famous Dom (see p014) and the Rathaus (see p064) of course, but also Romanesque churches, designer shopping and myriad museums such as the Wallraf-Richartz (see p070).

LANDMARKS
THE SHAPE OF THE CITY SKYLINE

Two of the most dramatic features of Cologne's skyline – the twin Gothic spires of Kölner Dom (see p014) and the sparkling 165m Köln Turm (overleaf) – are apt symbols for a city with a history spanning 1,000 years, but one that prides itself on being thoroughly modern. The Dom's stately presence is especially poignant given the Allied air raids during WWII, which decimated Cologne to the point that chief reconstruction architect Rudolf Schwarz called the city the 'world's greatest heap of rubble'. Another notable survivor was Jacob Koerfer's Hansahochhaus (Hansaring 97), which became one of the tallest buildings in Europe in 1925. The city's current highest structure, the 266m Colonius telecoms tower (Innere Kanalstrasse 100), has a viewing platform from which you can see over the Rhine to Deutz, where the 103m Köln Triangle (Ottoplatz 1, T 0221 8273 2989), a glass tower in the shape of a Reuleaux triangle, was unveiled in 2005. East and west banks are linked by the heavy-duty latticed steel superstructure of the Hohenzollernbrücke.

Dusseldorf has its own telecoms tower, the 240.5m Rheinturm (Stromstrasse 20), decorated with a light sculpture by Horst H Baumann; on a clear day, you can see Cologne from the observation deck. But the city's real symbols are Eller Maier Walter's showy 1988 Landtag state parliament (Platz des Landtags 1) and Frank Gehry's cartoon-like ensemble (see p012) in the arts and media harbour. *For full addresses, see Resources.*

Köln Turm

Jean Nouvel won the contest to design the 165m Cologne Tower, and it was unveiled in 2001 as the centrepiece of the vast MediaPark, a former freight depot turned playground for the digital generation. The natural reflective qualities of the double-glazed facade are compounded by images of clouds and local landmarks (including the Dom) that are etched on to enamel within the glass. A light installation by artist Heinz Mack gives it visual impact at night. There's no official lookout station, but the Osman30 restaurant (T 0221 5005 2080) on the 30th floor has a terrace, great Mediterranean cuisine and a lovely wine salon. While at MediaPark, check out the photography exhibitions in the SK Stiftung Kultur foundation (T 0221 888 950).
MediaPark 8, T 0221 5005 2000, www.koelnturm.de

Herkules Hochhaus

One of Cologne's most controversial buildings, the 102m Herkules High House is clad in blue, red, orange and violet enamel plates – winning the tower the affectionate nickname 'Papageien' (Parrot). Architect Peter Neufert, whose father, Ernst, was prominent in the Bauhaus School, envisaged it as 'super-house'; a high-rise complex spread over 31 floors and three basement levels, with a pool, sauna and solarium. Considered state-of-the-art at its unveiling in 1973, by the 1990s the tower had fallen into disrepair. Since a renovation programme began in 2005, including a €2.5m makeover of the facade, the Parrot has proudly displayed its bright plumage once again.
Graeffstrasse 1,
www.herkules-hochhaeuser.de

Der Neue Zollhof

Frank Gehry borrowed heavily from his misshapen Ginger & Fred building in Prague for the design of the 1999 Rheinhafen arts and media centre. The three building clusters rest on an expansive plaza, part of Dusseldorf's harbourside regeneration. They are constructed of concrete, but the finish on each is different: the east (white) buildings are composed of curvilinear volumes finished in plaster; the irregularly angled west (red) complex is clad in brick; and the central structure in metal – the reflection of the outer two groups on its skin, and the identical window units used throughout, unite the ensemble.

Stromstrasse 26

Kölner Dom

It is rumoured the Allies couldn't bring themselves to destroy Cologne's Gothic masterpiece. The cathedral, which stands 157m tall, is far more than an orientation point. Construction began in 1248 and took more than six centuries – it was finished in 1880, after the rediscovery of the original plan for the facade, thanks to new building techniques, such as the use of iron girders in the roof. The Dom was built to receive the increasing number of pilgrims making their way to the city to view the relics of the Three Magi, brought to Cologne in 1164 by Archbishop Rainald von Dasse. Look also for the Gero-Kreuz, an oak crucifix carved around 976AD, and the 11,263-piece stained-glass window by artist Gerhard Richter, unveiled in 2007. *Dompropstei, Margarethenkloster 5, T 0221 1794 0200, www.koelner-dom.de*

Kranhauser

The striking Crane Houses are the flagship in the redevelopment of Cologne's 1898 goods harbour. Designed by Hamburg architects Bothe Richter Teherani and inspired by El Lissitzky's Wolkenbügel, the three L-shaped glass-and-steel office and residential blocks, completed in 2009, mirror the cranes that used to dot this area. Around a third of the original harbour buildings remain, including the grain-storage houses, one of which been transformed into the Kunsthaus Rhenania (Bayenstrasse 28), a collective of 50 artists' studios that holds exhibitions. Also worth a detour is the double-trapezoid RheinauArtOffice (Holzmarkt 2a), by architects Freigeber and Stephan Schütt, home to Microsoft since 2008.
Harry-Blum-Platz 2,
www.rheinauhafen-koeln.de

HOTELS

WHERE TO STAY AND WHICH ROOMS TO BOOK

As Cologne's design and art scenes have grown, so has the choice of chic accommodation. With a constant stream of conference delegates, the city never had to try too hard, but even the grande dame Excelsior Ernst (Trankgasse 1-5, T 0221 2701), which has stood next to the Dom since 1863, underwent a €7m refurb to counter the increased competition. These days, you can book into the Andrée Putman-designed Hotel im Wasserturm (see p024); the Günnewig Stadtpalais (Deutz-Kalker-Strasse 52, T 0221 880 420), a modern reworking of the Kaiser Wilhelm Bad spa; a Big Apple-inspired loft (see p022); or one of the Hopper Group's triumvirate, perhaps the Et Cetera (Brüsseler Strasse 26, T 0221 924 400), fashioned out of a 19th-century monastery – rooms have parquet floors and cherry wood furnishings. Some of the most interesting newcomers cater to those on a budget, notably Die Wohngemeinschaft (opposite), and Marsil (Marsilstein 27, T 0221 469 0960), run by local creatives, offering 10 stylish apartments with kitchenettes in a listed house.

Despite its reputation as one of Germany's fashion capitals, hip accommodation is hard to come by in Dusseldorf. Try one of the Radissons (see p021) or the Burns Art Hotel (Bahnstrasse 76, T 0211 779 2910), set in a turn-of-the-century mansion. Its modern rooms and apartments have original stone floors and are decorated with sculpture; the Suite Maisonette is one of the best keys in town. *For full addresses and room rates, see Resources.*

Die Wohngemeinschaft

This funky eight-room hostel is a budget option, yet packs in enough imagination to stand with the heavyweights. It was born of the downstairs Wohngemeinschaft bar, a retro space with a VW Camper installation that's been catering to the hip local crowd since 2009. Each room here is designed around characters dreamt up by the owners. Telma (overleaf), for example, is dedicated to a Reykjavik art graduate, hence the *Wald vor lauter Bäumen* (forest full of trees) artwork and glacial feel, while Mikkel (above) is a Lego-inspired studio apartment. Sure, it's a novelty, but the original concept, and the basement theatre (next to the bar) that hosts gigs, readings and performances, make this a unique and lively place to stay. *Richard-Wagner-Strasse 39, T 0221 3976 0904, www.hostel-wohngemeinschaft.de*

Telma, Die Wohngemeinschaft

Radisson Blu

One of the most stylish business options in the city, Radisson Blu's Cologne venture is a large, glass-heavy hotel. Rooms have a contemporary feel, with clean lines, splashes of colour and stone-floored bathrooms, as seen in the Junior Suites (above). The Paparazzi restaurant serves Italian cuisine and has a brick-fired oven, and the lounge-bar (opposite) in the atrium, characterised by iron girders and huge pendant lights, is often used for fashion events. There are also two Radisson hotels in Dusseldorf – the Scandinavian (T 0211 45 530), which has a spa with indoor pool and a garden beside the Rheinpark, and the Media Harbour (T 0211 311 1910), with elegant interiors designed by Matteo Thun, and a good Italian restaurant, the Amano. *Messe-Kreisel 3, T 0221 277 200, www.radissonblu.com*

The New Yorker
This stylish hotel, designed by owner/
architect Johannes J Adams, has 40
chic rooms, but we recommend you
stay in the separate Boarding House,
in one of the five oak-floored lofts with
a Scandi design ethic (No 3: pictured).
The maze-like building also has a Finnish
sauna, library, gardens and a nightclub.
Deutz-Mülheimer Strasse 204,
T 0221 47 330, www.thenewyorker.de

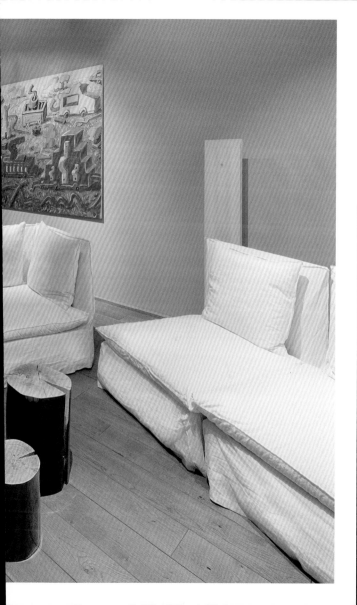

Hotel im Wasserturm

Cologne's most architecturally interesting place to lay your head occupies what was once the largest water tower in Europe. The 1872 structure was converted into a hotel in 1990, and transformed in 2007 by Andrée Putman, who added art by Andy Warhol, Jörg Immendorff, Wolfgang Tolk and Robert Rauschenberg, and decorated the necessarily curvy rooms with custom furnishings and tiled mosaics in the bathrooms. There's plenty of room to spread out too – Deluxe Suites (610; above) have 85 sq m of space and even Junior Suites (1001; opposite) boast a full 50 sq m. On the fifth floor is a sauna and the Atelier Beaut spa, but the pièce de résistance is the top-floor La Vision restaurant, the domain of chef Hans Horberth, which has a Michelin star and a terrace with panoramic views of the city.
Kaygasse 2, T 0221 20 080,
www.hotel-im-wasserturm.de

Savoy

Behind its drab exterior, the Savoy is full-on bling, designed by owner Gisela Ragge in conjunction with Austrian artist Andreas Reimann, whose collages infuse the hotel from the downstairs Diva bar to the rooms. Every floor has a theme – New York, Paris, Asia – within which each class of room has its own shape and style, though all have large beds, rich furnishings, plenty of texture, original artworks and a whirlpool. Almost like a love hotel gone kosher, the Savoy is not for the fainthearted, although the nudge-and-a-wink kitsch is rather fun for straight-laced Cologne. Surprisingly, the James Bond suites (pictured) are the most restrained. In the basement, the hotel has one of the city's best spas. *Turiner Strasse 9, T 0221 16 230, www.savoy.de*

Art'otel

This new-build by Viennese architect Johanne Nalbach opened in 2010 in the Rheinauhafen. Its art is by SEO, a Korean protégée of Georg Baselitz, and her subtly textured collages, many made from rice paper, adorn the exposed concrete of the lobby (opposite) and Pan-Asian restaurant Chino Latino. The 218 minimal rooms have original touches, such as tapered sinks and SEO reproductions printed on glass in the bathrooms. The Panorama and Corner rooms (501; above) have views over the Rhine, as many cantilever out of the facade; glass boxes located at irregular intervals that lend interest to what would otherwise be a simple rectangle. A roof terrace and bespoke furniture are further draws, although despite its best creative intentions, the Art'otel still comes across as rather corporate.
Holzmarkt 4, T 0221 801 030,
www.artotels.com

Hotel Chelsea

Opened in 1985, the Chelsea's incarnation as the city's original art hotel came about when its owner, Dr Werner Peters, made a drunken agreement with local artist Martin Kippenberger: a drawing for a free room. Kippenberger adopted the hotel as his home, paying for his digs in kind, and other artists followed suit, including Walter Dahn, Andreas Schulze and Rosemarie Trockel. The building is a nondescript 1960s concrete block, though 2001 saw the addition of a deconstructed roof extension by architect Hartmut Gruhl, with interiors by Casino Container. It houses seven angular rooms, most with a terrace, including the split-level Kippenberger Suite (right), which has a glass staircase that juts out of the facade. The Chelsea's most recent acquisition was a wall drawing by Turner Prize winner Richard Wright. *Jülicher Strasse 1, T 0221 207 150, www.hotel-chelsea.de*

24 HOURS
SEE THE BEST OF THE CITIES IN JUST ONE DAY

Cologne and Dusseldorf have a surprising wealth of contemporary art museums as well as a vibrant café culture and kicking nightlife. Start with the obvious – a nose around Cologne Cathedral (see p014) and the next-door Ludwig Museum (Heinrich-Böll-Platz, T 0221 26 165), by architects Peter Busmann and Godfried Haberer, which has an excellent Picasso collection. Also in Altstadt are the superb Angewandte Kunst (see p034) and Kolumba (see p036) museums.

After a morning of culture, head to Dusseldorf, stopping off on the way at art deco wonderland Norbert Esser (Poststrasse 12-14, T 0221 682 442), a warehouse packed with vintage lights, furniture and glassware. Reserve a table for lunch at Lido (see p040) and visit art meccas K20 and K21 (see p041) before an aperitif at the InterContinental's Bar 59 (Königsallee 59, T 0211 8285 1210).

In the evening, head back to Cologne's Belgian Quarter, where you'll find hip hangouts such as Hallmackenreuther (see p049) and Salon Schmitz (see p054). For dinner, get a feel for the city in a neighbourhood eaterie such as Kleines Schwarzes (see p045) or sample the local grapes at Wein Am Rhein (see p056). And forget about a good night's sleep; bars such as Six Pack (see p044) and Roxy (see p062), and dance palaces Studio 672 (Venloer Strasse 40, T 0221 952 9940) and Club Bahnhof Ehrenfeld (Bartholomäus-Schink-Strasse 65-67, T 0221 5309 8880), push on until dawn. *For full addresses, see Resources.*

09.00 Bastians

All-day café Bastians is renowned for its quality artisan breads and cakes, which are baked on the premises. The pleasant main space is simple, with untreated wood furniture, photography on the walls and diffused natural light. The breakfast menu runs from super-healthy dishes to the almost overwhelming Bastians Special (smoked salmon, a basket of German breads, cold cuts and scrambled eggs).

During the day, the specials are scrawled on a blackboard, anything from rye-bread lasagne to schnitzel. As an alternative, the tiny Café Café nearby (T 0221 270 6639) has a great range of bio food and a vivid colour scheme to wake you up. The original Bastians is in Dusseldorf, and is still going strong at Carlsplatz 24 (T 0211 863 9264). *Auf dem Berlich 3-5, T 0221 2508 3412, www.bastians-baecker.de*

10.00 Museum für Angewandte Kunst
Cologne's design museum was founded
in 1888 and is housed in a 1957
building by architect Rudolf Schwarz.
Temporary exhibitions, such as 'The
Art of Pop Video' (pictured), are held
in the main hall, while the permanent
collection is split into pre-1945 and
postwar. Highlights include Dieter
Rams' functionalist industrial designs.
An der Rechtschule, T 0221 2212 3860

11.00 Kolumba

Peter Zumthor's design for this museum incorporates the ruins of the late Gothic church St Kolumba, which was destroyed in WWII, save for a statue of the Virgin Mary around which Gottfried Böhm created his octagonal Madonna in the Ruins chapel in 1950 (opposite). The grey, rough-textured charcoal-fired brick, perforated in certain sections to allow in dappled light, works coherently with the stone of the remains on which it sits. Inside, a wooden walkway winds over excavated crypts, vaults and foundations. On the upper floors are 16 exhibition rooms housing an impressive permanent art collection that mixes early Christian masterpieces withcontemporary works by artists such as Richard Serra.
Kolumbastrasse 4, T 0221 933 1930, www.kolumba.de

12.30 Galerie Jablonka, Böhm Chapel
With his design of this 1956 church in the
town of Hürth on the southern outskirts
of Cologne, Gottfried Böhm created more
than a discreet nod to Henri Matisse's
chapel in Vence and Le Corbusier's church
at Ronchamp. The building consists of
a cupola resting on 24 pillars; under the
cedarwood shingled roof are six conches
with 8m-high windows decorated with
net-like iron grilles and a terrazzo floor.
The church was deconsecrated in 2006
and, since 2010, has served as a secular
exhibition space, run by Teresa and Rafael
Jablonka. Past shows have featured US
painter Terry Winters and 'Crystal Skull'
by Sherrie Levine (right). Beside the
chapel is a 24m-high campanile. The
gallery is open at weekends (times
vary) or by appointment.
*Hans-Böckler-Strasse 170, Hürth, T 0221
240 3426, www.jablonkagalerie.com*

15.00 Lido

There's plenty of architecture to admire in Dusseldorf's media harbour (see p012), not least this purpose-built steel-and-glass cube by local architects JSK, plopped in the middle of the water. Opened in 2005, the restaurant is anchored to the pedestrian bridge across the harbour. The main room seats 180 and has an interior kitted out in Californian walnut, while the lower level has a terrace that's so close to the water you can almost dip a toe in as you enjoy your digestif. Dynamic French cuisine is served courtesy of chef Florian Ohlmann – we recommend the lobster bisque, ox cheeks, and white nougat parfait with marinated wild berries. *Am Handelshafen 15, T 0211 1576 8730, www.lido1960.de*

16.30 K21

Dusseldorf's impressive state art collection was kickstarted in 1960 with the purchase of 88 works by Paul Klee, and is divided across two museums. K20 is housed in a 1986 granite building near the Hofgarten (Grabbeplatz 5) that was extended in 2010 by Danish architects Dissing+Weitling, and hosts Pollock, Rothko and the like in two pillar-free halls. About 1.5km away is K21 (above), opened in 2002 in the 1880

Ständehaus at Kaiserteich, the former seat of the provincial parliament. Architects Kiessler + Partner gutted the building bar the main staircase and replaced the roof with a glass cupola that houses a sculpture garden (overleaf). It displays art from the 1980s onwards, including work by Andreas Gursky, Sigmar Polke and Jeff Wall. *Ständehausstrasse 1, T 0211 838 1130, www.kunstsammlung.de*

Thomas Schütte's 'Big Spirits No 4 and 15' (right), sculpture garden, K21

20.00 Six Pack

One of the last survivors of Cologne's vibrant 1990s electronic music scene, before everyone split for Berlin, Six Pack has retained the grungy charm of its halcyon days. Fixed to the wall is an old vending machine that serves as a kind of museum for bizarre toys and objects, alongside an electric guitar and the odd poster or street-art piece. The long tubular bar is stocked with rows of bottled beers, including several varieties of the local Kölsch. Staff are reassuringly nonchalant and DJs spin everything from rock and hip hop to techno. While Six Pack is good for an early evening drink, it's usually pretty quiet before midnight – turn up around 4am to see the place in full swing with a mix of hipsters and night owls.
Aachener Strasse 33, T 0221 254 587

21.30 Kleines Schwarzes

Cologne is not blessed with a surfeit of fine dining, but there's a great vibe and cuisine at hip spot Little Black. Named after Coco Chanel's LBD, the restaurant opened in 2009 and offers inventive German and international cuisine in a smart space decorated with chandeliers, mirrors, grandfather clocks and velvet drapes. Chef Thomas Krüger's menu is full of surprises – the pepper soup has dabs of vanilla, guinea fowl breast is served with gnocchi – with an emphasis on regional, seasonal ingredients (the one dish served throughout the year is Breton fish soup). For a more formal evening affair, try Le Moissonnier (see p060) or the crisp white linen and rural French delicacies at Capricorn i Aries (T 0221 397 5710).
Klarastrasse 2, T 0221 562 6065,
www.kleinesschwarzes-koeln.de

23.30 Die Kunstbar

True to its name, Die Kunstbar (The Artbar) hands its keys over to an up-and-coming artist every year, giving them free rein to redesign everything, from the toilets to the bar menu. Since opening in 2008, guest designers have included Arne Quinze from Brussels, Joeressen+Kessner from Dusseldorf and locals Ingo Stein and Oliver Maichle. There are more than 100 cocktails on offer, including signature creations such as the Fizzer (gin, rum and rhubarb). The terrace seats 60 and has a lovely view of the Dom's looming spires, making this a scenic spot for a sundowner. Doors open at 8pm and there are DJs at weekends who pick the vibe up from 11pm. There's also live music every few weeks, and the place doesn't close until the last person leaves. Try to make sure it's not you.
Chargesheimerplatz 1, T 0172 527 9845, www.diekunstbar.com

URBAN LIFE

CAFÉS, RESTAURANTS, BARS AND NIGHTCLUBS

Cologne's restaurants might not be as decorated and its clubs not as decadent as elsewhere in Germany, but for a relatively small city, it has solid urban credentials. Restaurants such as Le Moissonnier (see p060), Capricorn i Aries (see p045) and La Vision (see p024) have all won Michelin stars, and Taku in the Excelsior Ernst (see p016) matches the best sushi in town with a minimal interior. These heavyweights are backed up by local eateries whose appeal lies in a delightful ambience and hearty food, among them Kleines Schwarzes (see p045), Feynsinn Café (see p052) and the excellent Italian Mercato Deluxe (Bremer Strasse 5, T 0221 139 9474).

There are plenty of cocktail haunts, such as the King Georg (Sudermanstrasse 2, T 0178 251 4896), an after-hours dive turned swanky bar that has kept its illicit vibe, with deep-red lighting. Equally popular, but rather brighter, is the all-white Ivory Lounge (Limburger Strasse 12, T 0221 277 4888) where, appropriately, it's as much about being seen as hitting the floor. Dusseldorf has its fair share of swagger, and Monkey's (Graf-Adolf-Platz 15, T 0211 6496 3711) and Nachtresidenz (see p059) attract a dressed-up clientele. In summer, Cologne's Rhein Terrassen (Rheinparkweg 1, T 0221 6500 4321) does a great weekend brunch beside the river, and Sky Beach (Cäcilienstrasse 32, T 0172 539 0567), is a slice of the Caribbean – complete with sand – on the ARAL car park roof. *For full addresses, see Resources.*

Hallmackenreuther

An established Belgian Quarter haunt of the city's graphic designers, architects and media types, Hallmackenreuther mixes 1950s and 1960s decor – Bakelite tabletops and lava lamps, plastic chairs and lights, some of which were sourced from the airport – with a modern outlook. A typical Cologne blend of café and bar, it's a convivial hangout at any time of day (open until 1am), and serves up international comfort food, such as salads, soups and pasta. There's a handsome upstairs lounge with a DJ set-up and the odd live performance. The huge front window opens up in summer, with outdoor seating on the pretty square beside St Michael's Church. *Brüsseler Platz 9, T 0221 517 970*

Elektra
Hidden away in the laidback residential district of Hansaring, Elektra has a retro-inspired interior that fits well with its soundtrack of funk, soul and house. The wood-panelled bar serves beers such as Rothaus Tannenzäpfle, a Pilsner-style lager brewed in Baden in the Black Forest, German wines and a few cocktails.
Gereonswall 12, T 0221 912 3832

Feynsinn Café

This refined café/bar has a Continental vibe. Large windows and mirrors allow light to flood the simple interior, which has a beautiful painted ceiling by Bettina Gruber (along with local sculptor David Smithson), who also designed the striking chandeliers crafted from glass shards. The kitchen serves up hearty breakfasts and Mediterranean dishes including the *Maultaschen*, a type of ravioli filled with minced meat and herbs. Many of the fresh produce comes from the owner's garden, and the excellent coffee is roasted on site. There's an extensive wine list, including Feynsinn's own Schwanengesang (white), which is custom-produced in Franken. The café's name is a play on *feinsinn*, which means gentle, sensitive, subtle.
Rathenauplatz 7, T 0221 240 9210, www.cafe-feynsinn.de

Brauhaus Päffgen

Bang in the heart of the nightlife strip Friesenstrasse, Päffgen has been making its own Kölsch since 1883 (it is the oldest brewery house in the city), and a convivial night here is a quintessentially Cologne experience. The place oozes old-school charm throughout. There is a series of rooms, including the Assembly Hall, lined with original wood panelling and vintage paintings; a winter garden (above), with crazy-paved tiling, a conservatory roof and a huge canvas depicting traditional brewing methods; intimate private rooms; and, of course, a beer garden. Line the stomach with the hearty Rhineland cuisine – try the *Halve Hahn* (literally 'half a chicken' but actually a rye roll with gouda and mustard), goulash or knuckle of pork. *Friesenstrasse 64, T 0221 135 461, www.paeffgen-koelsch.de*

Salon & Metzgerei Schmitz

Cologne's premier hangout has been drawing a hip crowd for more than a decade, and German artist Sigmar Polke, actor Daniel Brühl and director Lars von Trier have all dropped by. The interior features brick walls adorned with art – Salon Schmitz organises group shows during the Cologne Art Fair and solo exhibitions twice a year – and furniture is a mix of new and vintage. The best seats on a balmy summer evening are near the large window that opens on to the street. Food is prepared all day in the refurbished butcher's next door (Metzgerei), using organic regional produce. Popular orders are the schnitzel with potato salad, merguez sausages and the homemade cheesecake. By night, there's a real buzz about the place. You may well end up in the hidden Coco Schmitz club in the cellar.
Aachener Strasse 28, T 0221 139 5577, www.salonschmitz.com

Wein am Rhein
This smart, contemporary restaurant and wine emporium opened in 2009, with interiors by Annette Bartsch, who drew inspiration from the hill vineyards around her native Bad Neuenahr, well known for their reds. Her sketches were transformed into large carpets on the walls, the ceiling sculpture symbolises clouds and the Perspex chairs reference wine glasses. The cellar stocks more than 1,000 bottles, 30 of which are available by the glass. Sommeliers, including owner Mr Bouhs, are on hand to advise, and there are regular tastings and seminars. The refined international menu features dishes such as beef tartare with ricotta crostini, and there's a comprehensive tapas menu.
Johannisstrasse 64, T 0221 9124 8885,
www.weinamrhein.eu

Restaurant Hotel Hopper St Josef

The Hopper Group's St Josef hotel is a gem in sleepy Südstadt, fashioned out of a children's home that was set up in 1891 and extended in 1906. The real attraction here is the restaurant, which is beautifully sited in the former chapel, its interior an exercise in ecclesiastical chic, with vaulted ceilings, and chairs and tables that follow the ascetic theme without being plain. The international menu changes depending on the season, but isn't afraid to experiment. Say grace before tucking in to a potato and chorizo salad with rocket and lobster cream or Irish beef with sprouts and polenta.
Dreikönigenstrasse 1, T 0221 998 000, www.hopper.de

Nachtresidenz

A former theatre that dates from the early 1920s, Nachtresidenz has been reworked by designer Walter Henkenjohann into one of Dusseldorf's most stunning venues. Much of the original structure has been kept intact, and the high ceilings and bare-brick walls, accented by clever lighting, contrast well with the contemporary decor and slick styling. There are various areas, including a chillout lounge with a fireplace and a swanky Italian restaurant. At weekends, guest DJs such as Roger Sanchez and DJ Apl-De-Ap from The Black Eyed Peas play funky house and R&B to a switched-on crowd until 5am.
Bahnstrasse 13, T 0211 136 5755, www.nachtresidenz.de

Le Moissonnier

This French-style restaurant is one of Cologne's best. Founded in 1987 by sommelier Vincent Moissonnier, it has a traditional brasserie-style interior – mirrors, wood panelling, red leather banquettes, bentwood chairs and tiled floors – in which chef Eric Menchon, one of the few in the city to have won two Michelin stars, delivers his playful cuisine. Based loosely on French classics, roasted John Dory comes with lemon mascarpone muesli; rabbit loin is served with Thai bouillon and braised pak choi; and the cheeses are from Alsace. There are two wine lists: Les Sympathiques and Les Exceptionels. What makes Le Moissonnier special is not only the food but the warm, unpretentious atmosphere. *Krefelder Strasse 25, T 0221 729 479, www.lemoissonnier.de*

INSIDER'S GUIDE

LENA TERLUTTER, BOUTIQUE OWNER/FASHION BLOGGER

Style guru Lena Terlutter runs the Cologne blog Mode Junkies (www.modejunkies.blogspot.com) and owns Boutique Belgique (Brabanter Strasse 29, T 0163 845 5584), which she describes as a 'young concept store for every wallet'. Her perfect day would start with brunch at Salon & Metzgerei Schmitz (see p054) before browsing the nearby shops, such as Weekday (Ehrenstrasse 76-78, T 0221 2773 8670). For lunch, she loves Fischermanns (T 0221 2725 1920), inside multibrand store Apropos (see p080). 'I love to drink an Aperol spritz and watch people buying expensive clothes.' She might have a post-prandial coffee at Törtchen Törtchen (Alte Wallgasse 2a, T 0221 9987 9611), a cupcake shop dressed in pink.

Her favourite gallery is Arty Farty (Maastrichter Strasse 49, T 0221 1685 0055), which promotes young talent. 'It's all about art and wine – the best way to start any evening.' From here, Terlutter heads to Brüsseler Platz. 'Everyone meets there, in front of the church, having a beer.' For dinner, she suggests Bali (Brüsseler Platz 2, T 0221 522 914) or Warung Bayu (Brabanter Strasse 5, T 0221 589 4366), two Indonesian restaurants that represent the city's love affair with Asian food. On a big night she might head to Hallmackenreuther (see p049) or arty hangout Zum Goldenen Schuss (Antwerpener Strasse 38). She adds, 'If it's a long night, the last stop is the Roxy (Aachener Strasse 2, www.roxy.ag).'
For full addresses, see Resources.

ARCHITOUR

A GUIDE TO COLOGNE/DUSSELDORF'S ICONIC BUILDINGS

Given Cologne's razing by Allied forces during WWII, and its hasty reconstruction thereafter, the city can sometimes leave a little to be desired architecturally. There are, however, a decent amount of Roman and medieval remains, not least the church of Gross St Martin (Gross St Martin 9), constructed between 1150 and 1240, the Overstolzenhaus (opposite) and the 900-year-old Rathaus (Rathausplatz 2, T 0221 221 31 000), with Wilhelm Vernukken's Renaissance loggia and facade. Cologne also offers a smattering of contemporary structures by Pritzker Prize winners such as Gottfried Böhm and Lord Foster. Civic buildings like the Wallraf-Richartz Museum (see p070) and Peter Zumthor's Kolumba (see p036) bridge the gap, perfectly merging the ancient and modern.

Dusseldorf's churches and streets tend to be better preserved, due to less wartime bombardment. The city also boasts some 60 buildings designed by well-known architects, with much of the contemporary development taking place in the Arts and Media Harbour, including buildings by Frank Gehry (see p012) and David Chipperfield's Kaistrasse Studios. The Old Town boasts a mixed bag of delights, including the 1875 Opera House (Heinrich-Heine-Alle 24, T 0211 892 5211), the 1970 Schauspielhaus (see p066) and modern additions such as Christoph Ingenhoven's Sky Office (Kennedydam 24), an 89m tower encased in glass.

For full addresses, see Resources.

Overstolzenhaus

This magnificent example of secular Romanesque architecture was built in the early 13th century for the daughter of Gottschalk Overstolz, the patriarch of a merchant family. The first two floors of the house were residential, while the upper floors were used for storage. Heavily damaged in the war, the house was restored in 1955. It boasts a magnificent facade, complete with imposing gable, solid masonry and hints of early Gothic architecture in the large windows (those on the ground floor aren't original). Little of the interior has been preserved, but the first-floor banquet hall is still decorated with a 13th-century painting depicting a medieval tournament. The Overstolzenhaus currently houses the city's media college.
Rheingasse 8

Schauspielhaus

The distinctive ribbed concrete facade and nautical feel of Dusseldorf's main theatre was designed by local architect Bernhard Pfau. It was inaugurated in 1970 with a performance of Georg Büchner's *Danton's Death*, not without controversy – there was anger that no free tickets were offered, while the building itself was deemed elitist due to its 'closed' exterior (ironically Pfau had helped establish the Architektenring Dusseldorf in 1949 to protest that the top jobs were being handed to a 'former Nazi elite'). However, it has stood the test of time, and sits in harmony with the surrounding buildings, notably the angled slice of the 1960 Dreischeiben Hochhaus (left), designed by HPP.

Gustaf-Gründgens-Platz 1, T 0211 369 911, www.duesseldorfer-schauspielhaus.de

Tonhalle

This was the world's biggest planetarium when it opened in 1926 on the banks of the Rhine. Designed by Wilhelm Kreis, it featured a clinker brick facade and mosaics by expressionist Heinrich Nauen. It was converted into a 2,000-seat concert hall in 1978 by architect Helmut Hentrich, who preserved the shell, the decorative elements and the Grünes Gewölbe (Green Vault), with its exquisite glass collection.

In 2005, in order to counter the dome's echo, nicknamed the 'Klopfgeist' (knocking ghost), a transparent inner skin was added and acoustic reflectors and an integrated lighting system installed. The Tonhalle is the home of the Dusseldorf Symphony Orchestra, and has a diverse programme of more than 200 concerts a year.
Ehrenhof 1, T 0211 899 6123,
www.tonhalle-duesseldorf.de

Wallraf-Richartz-Museum

Late Cologne architect Oswald Mathias Ungers' Wallraf-Richartz Museum is a compelling blend of old and new. Opened in 1996, the building was constructed on a site that had lain empty since 1943, beside what was left of the Gothic church of Sankt Alban. The bulky basalt exterior features horizontal slits in place of large windows, and a trio of staggered blocks that echo the church bell tower. The museum displays European painting from the 13th to the 19th centuries, from the medieval Cologne artist Stefan Lochner's *Madonna of the Rose Bower* to an extensive collection of Dutch Masters and French impressionists. The basement gallery hosts temporary exhibitions among its ancient stone vaults.
Obenmarspforten, T 0221 221 119, www.wallraf.museum

Legal Illegal House

Manuel Herz's deconstructionalist creation appears defiant against its mundane surroundings in the southern suburb of Bayenthal. The property consists of a basement and ground-floor office, with two apartments above, the design maximising the narrow plot by squeezing in 400 sq m of real estate. Two starkly different volumes are superimposed on each other: one a virtually translucent rectangle that follows all planning regulations, the other a technically 'illegal' free-form polyurethane red shell. Support is garnered from the party walls of the neighbouring buildings. To compensate for the lack of horizontal space and to add light, each apartment has its own atrium.

Goltsteinstrasse 110, www.manuelherz.com

WDR-Arkaden

The HQ of broadcasting company WDR was designed by Pritzker Prize winner Gottfried Böhm in collaboration with his wife, Elizabeth, and opened in 1996. The imposing building comprises a series of rectangular glass boxes stacked on stilts at irregular angles to create 21,000 sq m of usable space. The street-level arcades are intended to connect the broadcasting company directly with the general public, and three passages lined with retail and restaurants lead into the centre of the building, an atrium topped by a glass dome. Local news reports are broadcast from the building on a daily basis.
6-26 Breite Strasse, www.wdr.de

Kölner Opernhaus
The 1962 opera house was designed by
Cologne architect Wilhelm Riphahn and is
undergoing extensive refurbishment. The
interior, where jazz pianist Keith Jarrett's
legendary *Köln Concert* was recorded,
was renovated by local firm JSWD in 2008.
The striking auditorium has 1,300 seats,
the best of which are suspended in vertical
terraces divided by giant wooden blocks.
Offenbachplatz, T 0221 221 8400

Gürzenich Ensemble

This collection of civic buildings stretches back almost six centuries. Built in the 1440s, it served as a court and a market hall before becoming a key address for city functions. Concerts performed here from 1857 were the foundation of Cologne's global reputation for musical excellence; Gustav Mahler conducted the Gürzenich Orchestra's premiere of his 5th Symphony in 1904. It was rebuilt after the war under the guidance of Rudolf Schwarz and Karl Band, and turned into a congress and events centre in 1997 by KSP Engel Kraemer Schmiedecke Zimmermann, who added the glass elevator to the exterior. The courtyard contains a reproduction of German expressionist Käthe Kollwitz's *The Grieving Parents* war memorial. *Martinstrasse 27-29, T 0221 821 2434, www.koelnkongress.de*

Weltstadthaus

Renzo Piano's bulbous Peek & Cloppenburg department store on busy Schildergasse arrived in 2005 and has been variously described as a whale, a waterfall and a bishop's mitre. The idiosyncratic facade rises 34m high and comprises 6,800 glass panels, almost all unique in curvature and dimensions, mounted in Siberian larch girders and supported by a reinforced concrete skeleton. The building also cleverly embraces its sloping site. Peek & Cloppenburg's flagship in Dusseldorf is similarly striking. Designed by New York architect Richard Meier, it is distinctive for its five-storey curved window – another ode to space and transparency. The transparency being, of course, the fact that P&C want you to spend your money. *Schildergasse 65-67, T 0221 421 3347, www.peek-cloppenburg.de*

Gerling-Areal

In 1920 Robert Gerling bought the Palais
von Langen as an HQ for his insurance
company. It was destroyed in the war and
the Gerling-Areal grew from the ashes.
Kurt Groote used the foundations for a
new building decorated with zodiac signs
and the sun (symbolism resonant with
both a bank and the Third Reich). Hentrich
and Heuser added the Gereonshof wings
and in 1953 the high-rise Hochhaus was
completed. The Rundbau (right), an open
rotunda designed by Franz Heinrich
Sobotka and Gustav Müller, arrived in
1966 and included the Hildeboldplatz.
The ensemble is united by the buildings'
bright shell-limestone facades and is a
superb example of postwar modernism.
The site was sold for redevelopment in
2005 and local architects KSG will add
a 'gate' to the Gereonshof and turn the
Hochhaus into luxury flats for 2013.
www.gerling-quartier.de

SHOPPING

THE BEST RETAIL THERAPY AND WHAT TO BUY

Cologne's key retail arteries are Hohe Strasse and Schildergasse, which leads to the distinctive Neumarkt mall, topped by artists Claes Oldenburg and Coosje van Bruggen's *Dropped Cone*. Nearby is Manufactum (Brückenstrasse 23, T 0221 2994 2323) inside Bruno Paul's expressionist Disch-Haus, from 1930, where you can find anything from ham-slicing machines to wellies. Within a short stroll are Renzo Piano's Peek & Cloppenburg (see p077); the concept store Apropros (Mittelstrasse 12, T 0221 272 5190), which sells Lala Berlin, Etro and Markus Lupfer; and the delightful bookshop Buchhandlung Walther König (Ehrenstrasse 4, T 0221 205 960). Brüsseler Platz and environs are home to a cluster of independent fashion stores, including Bob 10.5.10 (No 6, T 0221 1686 9348), Boutique Belgique (Brabanter Strasse 29, T 0163 845 5584) and Chang 13 (Maastrichter Strasse 19, T 0221 719 2613), which carries Cologne designers such as Eva Gronbach. In Deutz, Design Post (Deutz-Mülheimer Strasse 22a, T 0221 690 650) has more than 30 homewares brands from Europe under one roof.

Dusseldorf's reputation within Germany as a fashion hub may lead to disappointment, as it's founded not on local creativity but the preponderance of high-end global fashion brands, such as Chanel and Prada, clustered along the 'style mile', Königsallee. Department stores and design shops are on nearby Schadowstrasse. *For full addresses, see Resources.*

Utensil

Run by Cologne designer Anna Lederer, Utensil is one of several funky stores that have popped up along Körnerstrasse in Ehrenfeld. Touting 'simple' everyday products with an emphasis on long-lasting design, Lederer removes these wares from their usual workplace context and brings them into the domestic. The shop occupies a former butcher's and the shabby exterior was left intact, while the interior has been redesigned by local studio Halfmann Mennickheim, making a feature of the existing ceramic wall tiles. Arranged beautifully is everything from Duralex Picardie glassware to sailor raincoats by Friesennerz, laboratory dropper bottles repurposed as salad dressing holders and chairs by Xavier Pauchard.
Körnerstrasse 21, T 0221 1683 1673, www.utensil-shop.de

Jürgen Eifler

Walking into Jürgen Eifler's men's hat store is like going back in time. It first opened in 1984, but cramming every nook and cranny are the vintage hat boxes, advertisements, antique sewing machines and black-and-white photos that give it a centuries-old feel. Everything is done in the traditional way here. Eifler, who is from Cologne, trained in France, Belgium and Germany. All hats are made on site – out the back you can see staff working on the bowlers, workers' caps and homburgs – using top-quality materials, such as toquilla straw from Ecuador for the Superfino Panama hats. Order bespoke (as does Karl Lagerfeld) by picking a sample and the material; Eifler himself is often on hand to advise. It takes around a fortnight to make a hat and the store can mail you the finished article.
Friesenwall 102a, T 0221 254 535,
www.hut-classic.com

Herr von Eden

Classy German label Herr von Eden is inspired by 1930s British men's outfitters and has built up a reputation for its slim, tapered tailoring since starting out in 1998. The shop blends a contemporary interior with vintage display cases and wooden fittings. Its high-quality shirts and suits often come with a twist, such as an unexpectedly colourful silk polka-dot lining. There is also a womenswear collection, which retains a masculine feel, and a fine selection of handmade shoes. The service here is exemplary.
Antwerpener Strasse 6-12,
T 0221 589 2149, www.herrvoneden.com

Hernando Cortez Schokoladen
This small and unassuming chocolate shop and café was founded by Marco Mühlberg in 2007 and serves the best hot chocolate in town – there are no powdered grains used here, only rich butter and cocoa mixes. There's a fantastic range of the solid stuff from boutique European producers such as Bonnat, Domori, Valrhona and Bovetti. We recommend you try the French praline from Normandy's Michel Cluizel, one of Europe's most famous chocolatiers. With its warm interior, white-and-gold decor and Villeroy & Boch crockery, HCS is the perfect spot for a *gemütlich* break.
Gertrudenstrasse 23, T 0221 2725 0570, www.hernando-cortez.de

19 West Furniture

This delightful repository of vintage furniture is located in a 300 sq m warehouse building in the Köln-Mülheim harbour area. The owner, Jochen Kloeters, has sourced a fascinating collection of 20th-century classics by such names as Charles Eames, Friso Kramer, Egon Eiermann and Angelo Mangiarotti, plus re-editions and several contemporary pieces. On our visit we spied a 1950s modernist desk by Cees Braakman for Dutch manufacturer Pastoe, and a series of 'Boomerang' easy chairs, designed in 1953 by Hans Mitzlaff and Albrecht Lange for German maker Eugen Schmid. The bare-brick showroom is open by appointment only, but 19 West sells via its website and ships worldwide.
Gustav-Cords-Strasse 19,
T 0221 3799 0694, www.19west.de

SPORTS AND SPAS

WORK OUT, CHILL OUT OR JUST WATCH

Cologne and Dusseldorf are famous sporting rivals, and if there's a derby match on while you're in town, it's definitely worth getting tickets. Cologne's football team, FC Köln, were formed in 1948 and play at the RheinEnergieStadion (Aachener Strasse 999, T 0221 7161 6150), which holds 50,000 spectators and was a venue for the 2006 World Cup. Ice hockey fans can catch the Kölner Haie (Cologne Sharks) at the Lanxess Arena (opposite), but it's the Dusseldorf team – the DEG Metro Stars – who are the real draw, as they are one of the most successful sides in Germany. Home matches take place at the ISS Dome (Theodorstrasse 281, T 0211 892 7700).

Cologne has been famous for its spas since Roman times, an era that clearly served as an inspiration to Claudius Therme (Sachsenbergstrasse 1, T 0221 981 440), which is built in the style of Roman baths, with saunas, cold plunge pools, a steam bath, sanarium and gardens; the water comes from a thermal mineral spring. A more contemporary outlook can be found in Neptunbad (see p094) and Dusseldorf's Momentum Spa (see p092). Joggers head towards green spaces such as the Aachener Weiher, the Volksgarten or along the banks of Rhine. To kill two birds with one stone and orient oneself on a whistlestop tour, 'sightrunning' is popular in Germany – organise your dash through the city at www.koeln-sightjogging.de or www.run-and-see-duesseldorf.de. *For full addresses, see Resources.*

Lanxess Arena

Located on the east bank of the Rhine, the Lanxess Arena opened in 1998. Designed by Peter Böhm, son of Gottfried (see p038), the structure is dominated by a distinctive 76m steel arch, visible from right across town, which supports the roof. Underneath is a space the size of 12 football pitches, with state-of-the-art technology including a suspended 20-ton video cube and a watt-laden sound system. It can seat up to 18,000 spectators and is the largest events venue in Germany, hosting sport, concerts and conferences. *Willy-Brandt-Platz 3, T 0221 8021, www.lanxess-arena.de*

Winterberg

The ski resort of Winterberg is roughly two hours west of Cologne. Set in the forested mountain range Rothaargebirge, it has 30 pistes served by 23 lifts, many of them high capacity, plus snowmaking machines to counter the low altitude. The six mountains offer 7.5km of pistes – mostly easy and intermediate – a couple of toboggan runs and the St George ski jump. The latter, built in 1959 by Fritz Gladen, has an arch span of 43m and total length of 220m (the jump record of 89.5m was set in 2000 by Manuel Fettner). Fourteen of the pistes are floodlit for night skiing on Wednesdays, Fridays and Saturdays, and there is a party atmosphere as up to 50,000 German and Dutch skiers and snowboarders descend (literally) at weekends. Winterberg also has a luge and skeleton track, and its bobsleigh run (right) will host the 2015 world championships.
www.skiliftkarussell.de

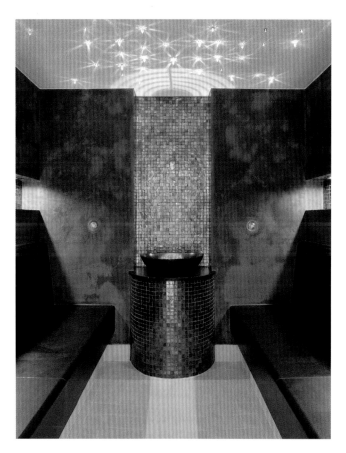

Momentum Spa

The centrepiece of this stylish spa in Dusseldorf, which opened in 2009, is a light-flooded 800 sq m relaxation area (opposite) with an elegant saltwater pool (a rarity in German spas). The interior features earthy tones, custom-made Italian tiles and Canadian wood. In the sauna area, there's a 'Starry Sky' of Swarovski stones with a steam room (above) and a shower area with a shell mosaic, tropical rain wall and ice tower. Its Symphony Spa bath tub, which can accommodate two people, combines classical music, pulsing magnetic fields and aromatherapy to provide a truly multi-sensory experience.

Am Bonneshof 30a, T 0211 518 0870, www.momentum-spa.de

Neptunbad
This Asian-inspired spa has been
fashioned out of a 1912 art nouveau pile.
Facilities include a sauna with Roman
laconium, a pool with gabled glass roof,
steam baths and a meditation pool with
underwater music. The Japanese garden
has two hot-water onsen baths; there are
rock pools and a fire pit for colder days.
*Neptunplatz 1, T 0221 710 071,
www.neptunbad.de*

ESCAPES

WHERE TO GO IF YOU WANT TO LEAVE TOWN

In the 1950s and 1960s, North Rhine-Westphalia – in particular the Ruhr – was one of the most important industrial regions in Europe, contributing directly to the German *Wirtschaftswunder* (economic miracle). Today, this area, an hour north of Cologne, is a compelling post-industrial landscape. A 400km heritage trail follows a circular route via 25 anchor points, including museums of social history and panoramic lookout stations. Of particular interest is Zollverein (opposite), once the most advanced coal pit in the world and now a highly successful regeneration project.

Those who prefer nature can go hiking or cycling through the woodlands of the Eifel National Park, or explore the low mountain ranges and lakes of Bergisches Land. For a cultural fix, head 25km south of Cologne to Bonn, the former capital of West Germany. Its Museum Mile connects the gloriously eccentric Art and Exhibition Hall (see p098) to the 1992 Kunstmuseum (Friedrich Ebert Allee 2, T 0228 776 260), which presents an excellent collection of Rhenish expressionist and postwar German art, including work by Max Ernst, Joseph Beuys, Gerhard Richter and Georg Baselitz, in a beautifully light, geometrical space realised by architect Axel Schultes. From here, continue down the Rhine past classic German castles such as Stolzenfels (see p100) and on to Mainz, where Manuel Herz's Jewish Community Centre (see p102) is a modern architectural gem. *For full addresses, see Resources.*

Zollverein, Essen

This UNESCO World Heritage Site has been dubbed 'the world's most beautiful coal mine'. The last of the black stuff was extracted in 1986, and the site has been transformed into a cultural centre based on a masterplan by OMA, with former rail tracks and sky bridges now public walkways. The Boiler House was turned into the Red Dot Design Museum (T 0201 301 040) by Lord Foster in 1997 and the Coal Washing Plant, the largest surface building at Zollverein, was converted into the Ruhr Museum (T 0201 2468 1444) by Rem Koolhaas. In 2006, a new-build was added – SANAA's Zollverein School, an arresting white cube with 134 irregular windows that provide unusual perspectives over the whole site.
Gelsenkirchenerstrasse 181,
T 0201 246 810, www.zollverein.de

FRG Art and Exhibition Hall, Bonn
Viennese architect Gustav Peichl's
museum opened in 1992, unmistakable
for its whimsy, notably the three
huge blue pointed cones on its roof,
surrounded by a sculpture garden with
views over the Rhine Valley. Underneath
is 5,600 sq m of exhibition space, and
concerts and events are held year round.
*Friedrich-Ebert-Allee, T 0228 91 710,
www.kah-bonn.de*

Schloss Stolzenfels, Koblenz

North Rhine-Westphalia doesn't have the same wealth of historic castles as other regions in Germany. However, it's worth the hour's trip to Koblenz to visit Stolzenfels, perched high above the Rhine. Like other structures along the river, it began life, in the 13th century, as a glorified toll station but was destroyed by the invading French in 1689. The ruins were presented to King Friedrich Wilhelm by the city of Koblenz and it was rebuilt as a summer residence between 1835 and 1845 in the English Tudor style, with ochre walls, pergolas and terraces, to plans drawn up by the master Prussian architect Karl Friedrich Schinkel. The interior is richly furnished with works of art and wall paintings, including some of the most important works of Rhine romanticism.
T 0261 51 656, www.schloss-stolzenfels.de

Indemann, Inden

Since the 1990s, several villages in Inden have had to be relocated to make way for what is now a 4,500-hectare opencast lignite mine, resulting in a surreal, pitted landscape. This symbolic watchman, next to the autobahn between Aachen and Cologne, alludes to the colossal excavators that dot the area, and only adds to the otherworldly feel of the place. Designed by Maastricht firm MUA to signal the 'social revival of a non-urban space', the 36m glass-and-steel 'robot' extends its arm over the scarred earth, and stairs lead to a series of viewing platforms. The Indemann's front contains 40,000 LEDs, which display artists' animations, allowing the structure to act as a contemporary lighthouse. In 2030, when excavation ends, the area will become a watersports and recreation park. *Goldsteinkuppe, T 0246 53 961*

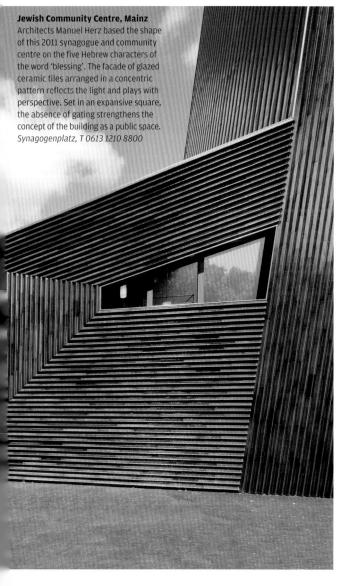

Jewish Community Centre, Mainz
Architects Manuel Herz based the shape
of this 2011 synagogue and community
centre on the five Hebrew characters of
the word 'blessing'. The facade of glazed
ceramic tiles arranged in a concentric
pattern reflects the light and plays with
perspective. Set in an expansive square,
the absence of gating strengthens the
concept of the building as a public space.
Synagogenplatz, T 0613 1210 8800

NOTES
SKETCHES AND MEMOS

RESOURCES

CITY GUIDE DIRECTORY

A

Apropos 080
Mittelstrasse 12
T 0221 272 5190
www.apropos-store.com

Arty Farty 062
Maastrichter Strasse 49
T 0221 1685 0055
www.artyfarty-gallery.com

B

Bali 062
Brüsseler Platz 2
T 0221 522 914

Bar 59 032
Königsallee 59
T 0211 8285 1210
www.duesseldorf.intercontinental.com

Bastians Cologne 033
Auf dem Berlich 3-5
T 0221 2508 3412
www.bastians-baecker.de

Bastians Dusseldorf 033
Carlsplatz 24
T 0211 863 9264
www.bastians-baecker.de

Bob 10.5.10 080
Brüsseler Platz 6
T 0221 1686 9348
www.bob10510.de

Boutique Belgique 062
Brabanter Strasse 29
T 0163 845 5584
boutiquebelgique.blogspot.com

Brauhaus Päffgen 053
Friesenstrasse 64
T 0221 135 461
www.paeffgen-koelsch.de

Buchhandlung Walther König 080
Ehrenstrasse 4
T 0221 205 960
www.buchhandlung-walther-koenig.de

C

Café Café 033
Aachener Strasse 45
T 0221 270 6639
www.cafecafe.de

Capricorn i Aries 045
Alteburgerstrasse 34
T 0221 397 5710
www.capricorniaries.com

Chanel 080
Königsallee 30
T 0211 325 935
www.chanel.com

Chang 13 080
Maastrichter Strasse 19
T 0221 719 2613
www.chang13.com

Claudius Therme 088
Sachsenbergstrasse 1
T 0221 981 440
www.claudius-therme.de

Club Bahnhof Ehrenfeld 032
Bartholomäus-Schink-Strasse 65-67
T 0221 5309 8880
cbe-cologne.de

Colonius 009
Innere Kanalstrasse 100

D

Design Post 080
Deutz-Mülheimer Strasse 22a
T 0221 690 650
www.designpostkoeln.de

E
Elektra 050
Gereonswall 12
T 0221 912 3832

F
Federal Republic of Germany Art & Exhibition Hall 098
Friedrich-Ebert-Allee
Bonn
T 0228 91 710
www.kah-bonn.de
Feynsinn Café 052
Rathenauplatz 7
T 0221 240 9210
www.cafe-feynsinn.de
Fischermanns 062
Apropos
Mittelstrasse 12
T 0221 2725 1920
www.restaurant-fischermanns.de

G
Galerie Jablonka 038
Böhm Chapel
Hans-Böckler-Strasse 170
Hürth
T 0221 240 3426
www.jablonkagalerie.com
Gerling-Areal 078
Von Werth Strasse 1
www.gerlingquartier.de
Gross St Martin 064
Gross St Martin 9
www.romanische-kirchen-koeln.de
Gürzenich Ensemble 076
Martinstrasse 27-29
T 0221 821 2434
www.koelnkongress.de

H
Hallmackenreuther 049
Brüsseler Platz 9
T 0221 517 970
Hansahochhaus 009
Hansaring 97
Herkules Hochhaus 011
Graeffstrasse 1
www.herkules-hochhaeuser.de
Hernando Cortez Schokoladen 085
Gertrudenstrasse 23
T 0221 2725 0570
www.hernando-cortez.de
Herr von Eden 084
Antwerpener Strasse 6-12
T 0221 589 2149
www.herrvoneden.com

I
Indemann 101
Goldsteinkuppe
Inden
T 0246 53 961
ISS Dome 088
Theodorstrasse 281
T 0211 892 7700
www.issdome.de
Ivory Lounge 048
Limburger Strasse 12
T 0211 277 4888
www.ivorylounge.de

J
Jewish Community Centre 102
Synagogenplatz
Mainz
T 06131 210 8800
www.jgmainz.de

Jürgen Eifler 082
Friesenwall 102a
T 0221 254 535
www.hut-classic.com

K
K20 041
Grabbeplatz 5
T 0211 838 1130
www.kunstsammlung.de
K21 041
Ständehausstrasse 1
T 0211 838 1130
www.kunstsammlung.de
Kaistrasse Studios 064
Kaistrasse 16-18
King Georg 048
Sudermanstrasse 2
T 0178 251 4896
www.kinggeorg.de
Kleines Schwarzes 045
Klarastrasse 2
T 0221 562 6065
www.kleinesschwarzes-koeln.de
Köln Triangle 009
Ottoplatz 1
T 0221 8273 2989
www.kolntriangle.de
Köln Turm 010
MediaPark 8
T 0221 5005 2000
www.koelnturm.de
Kölner Dom 014
Dompropstei
Margarethenkloster 5
T 0221 1794 0555
www.koelner-dom.de

Kölner Opernhaus 074
Offenbachplatz
T 0221 2212 8400
www.operkoeln.com
Kolumba 036
Kolumbastrasse 4
T 0221 933 1930
www.kolumba.de
Kranhauser 015
Harry-Blum Platz 2
www.rheinauhafen-koeln.de
Die Kunstbar 046
Chargesheimerplatz 1
T 0172 527 9845
www.diekunstbar.com
Kunsthaus Rhenania 015
Bayenstrasse 28
www.rhenaniakunsthaus.de
Kunstmuseum Bonn 096
Friedrich Ebert Allee 2
T 0228 776 260
www.kunstmuseum-bonn.de

L
Landtag state parliament 009
Platz des Landtags 1
T 0211 8840
www.landtag.nrw.de
Lanxess Arena 089
Willy-Brandt-Platz 3
T 0221 8021
www.lanxess-arena.de
Legal Illegal House 072
Goltsteinstrasse 110
www.manuelherz.com
Lido 040
Am Handelshafen 15
T 0211 1576 8730
www.lido1960.de

Ludwig Museum 032
Heinrich-Böll-Platz
T 0221 26 165
www.museum-ludwig.de

M
Manufactum 080
Brückenstrasse 23
T 0221 2994 2323
www.manufactum.de
Mercato Deluxe 048
Bremer Strasse 5
T 0221 139 9474
www.mercato-deluxe.de
Le Moissonnier 060
Krefelder Strasse 25
T 0221 729 479
www.lemoissonnier.de
Momentum Spa 092
Am Bonneshof 30a
Dusseldorf
T 0211 518 0870
www.momentum-spa.de
Monkey's 048
Graf-Adolf-Platz 15
T 0211 6496 3711
www.monkeysplaza.com
Museum für Angewandt Kunst 034
An der Rechtschule
T 0221 2212 3860
www.makk.de

N
19 West Furniture 086
Gustav-Cords-Strasse 19
T 0221 3799 0694
www.19west.de

Nachtresidenz 059
Bahnstrasse 13
T 0211 136 5755
www.nachtresidenz.de
Neptunbad 094
Neptunplatz 1
T 0221 710 071
www.neptunbad.de
Der Neue Zollhof 012
Stromstrasse 26
Norbert Esser 032
Poststrasse 12-14
T 0221 682 442
esserartdeco.de

O
Opera House Dusseldorf 064
Heinrich-Heine-Allee 24
T 0211 892 5211
www.rheinoper.de
Osman30 010
Köln Turm
MediaPark 8
T 0221 5005 2080
www.osman-cologne.de
Overstolzenhaus 065
Rheingasse 8

P
Prada 080
Königsallee 34a
T 0211 865 780
www.prada.com

R
Rathaus 064
Rathausplatz 2
T 0221 221 31 000
Red Dot Design Museum 097
Zollverein
Gelsenkirchener Strasse 181
Essen
T 0201 301 040
www.red-dot.de
Restaurant Hotel Hopper St Josef 058
Dreikönigenstrasse 1
T 0221 998 000
www.hopper.de
RheinauArtOffice 015
Holzmarkt 2a
RheinEnergieStadion 088
Aachener Strasse 999
T 0221 7161 6150
www.fc-koeln.de
Rhein Terrassen 048
Rheinparkweg 1
T 0221 6500 4321
www.rhein-terrassen.de
Rheinturm 009
Stromstrasse 20
Roxy 062
Aachener Strasse 2
www.roxy.ag
Ruhr Museum 097
Zollverein
Gelsenkirchen Strasse 181
Essen
T 0201 2468 1444
www.ruhrmuseum.de

S
Salon & Metzgerei Schmitz 054
Aachener Strasse 28
T 0221 139 5577
www.salonschmitz.com
Schauspielhaus 066
Gustaf-Gründgens-Platz 1
T 0211 369 911
www.duesseldorf-schauspielhaus.de
Schloss Stolzenfels 100
Koblenz
T 0261 51656
www.schloss-stolzenfels.de
Six Pack 044
Aachener Strasse 33
T 0221 254 587
SK Stiftung Kultur 010
MediaPark 7
T 0221 888 950
www.sk-kultur.de
Sky Beach 048
Cäcilienstrasse 32
T 0172 539 0567
www.skybeach.de
Sky Office 064
Kennedydam 24
www.skyoffice.de
Studio 672 032
Venloer Strasse 40
T 0221 952 9940
www.stadtgarten.de

T
Taku 048
Excelsior Ernst
Trankgasse 1
T 0221 270 3910
www.taku.de

Tonhalle 068
 Ehrenhof 1
 T 0211 899 6123
 www.tonhalle-duesseldorf.de
Törtchen Törtchen 062
 Alte Wallgasse 2a
 T 0221 9987 9611
 www.toertchentoertchen.de

U
Utensil 081
 Körnerstrasse 21
 T 0221 1683 1673
 www.utensil-shop.de

V
La Vision 024
 Kaygasse 2
 T 0221 200 80
 www.hotel-im-wasserturm.de

W
Wallraf-Richartz-Museum 070
 Obenmarspforten
 T 0221 221 119
 www.wallraf.museum
Warung Bayu 062
 Brabanter Strasse 5
 T 0221 589 4366
 www.warungbayu.de
WDR-Arkaden 073
 6-26 Breite Strasse
 www.wdr.de
Weekday 062
 Ehrenstrasse 76-78
 T 0221 277 38670
 www.weekday.com

Wein am Rhein 056
 Johannisstrasse 64
 T 0221 9124 8885
 www.weinamrhein.eu
Weldstadthaus 077
 Schildergasse 65-67
 T 0221 421 3347
 www.peek-cloppenburg.de

Z
Zollervein 097
 Gelsenkirchenerstrasse 181
 Essen
 T 0201 246 810
 www.zollverein.de
Zum Goldenen Schuss 062
 Antwerpener Strasse 38

HOTELS
ADDRESSES AND ROOM RATES

Art'otel 028
Room rates:
double, from €89;
Art Corner Room 501, €149;
Panorama Room, €229
Holzmarkt 4
T 0221 801 030
www.artotels.com

Burns Art Hotel 016
Room rates:
double, from €175;
apartments, from €165;
Suite Maisonette, €198
Bahnstrasse 76
T 0211 779 2910
www.hotel-burns.de

Hotel Chelsea 030
Room rates:
double, from €93;
Kippenberger Suite, €195
Jülicher Strasse 1
T 0221 207 150
www.hotel-chelsea.de

Excelsior Hotel Ernst 016
Room rates:
double, from €210
Trankgasse 1-5
T 0221 2701
www.excelsiorhotelernst.de

Günnewig Stadtpalais 016
Room rates:
double, from €99
Deutz-Kalker-Strasse 52
T 0221 880 420
www.guennewig.de

Hopper Hotel Et Cetera 016
Room rates:
double, from €145
Brüsseler Strasse 26
T 0221 924 400
www.hopper.de

Marsil 016
Room rates:
double, from €88
Marsilstein 27
T 0221 4690 960
www.marsil.de

The New Yorker 022
Room rates:
double, €125;
Loft No 3, €165
Deutz-Mülheimer Strasse 204
Cologne
T 0221 47 330
www.thenewyorker.de

Radisson Blu 020
Room rates:
double, from €145;
Junior Suite, €250
Messe Kreisel 3
T 0221 277 200
www.radissonblu.com

Radisson Blu Media Harbour 021
Room rates:
double, from €130
Hammer Strasse 23
T 0221 311 1910
www.radissonblu.com

Radisson Blu Scandinavian Hotel 021
Room rates:
double, from €150
Karl-Arnold-Platz 5
Dusseldorf
T 0211 45 530
www.radissonblu.com

Savoy 026
Room rates:
double, from €197;
James Bond Suite, €553
Turiner Strasse 9
T 0221 16 230
www.savoy.de

Hotel im Wasserturm 024
Room rates:
double, from €190;
Junior Suite, from €225;
Deluxe Suite 610, from €485
Kaygasse 2
T 0221 20 080
www.hotel-im-wasserturm.de

Die Wohngemeinschaft 017
Room rates:
double, from €59;
Telma, €89;
Mikkel, price on request
Richard-Wagner-Strasse 39
T 0221 3976 0904
www.hostel-wohngemeinschaft.de

WALLPAPER* CITY GUIDES

Executive Editor
Rachael Moloney

Editor
Jeremy Case
Author
Paul Sullivan

Art Director
Loran Stosskopf

Art Editor
Eriko Shimazaki
Designer
Mayumi Hashimoto
Map Illustrator
Russell Bell

Photography Editor
Sophie Corben
Deputy Photography Editor
Anika Burgess
Photography Assistant
Nabil Butt

Chief Sub-Editor
Nick Mee
Sub-Editors
Greg Hughes
Matt Sinha

Editorial Assistant
Emma Harrison

Interns
Claudia Chwalisz
Peter Maxwell

**Wallpaper* Group
Editor-in-Chief**
Tony Chambers
Publishing Director
Gord Ray
Managing Editor
Jessica Diamond

Contributor
Kristina Raderschad

Wallpaper* ® is a
registered trademark
of IPC Media Limited

First published 2012

All prices are correct at
the time of going to press,
but are subject to change.

Printed in China

PHAIDON

Phaidon Press Limited
Regent's Wharf
All Saints Street
London N1 9PA

Phaidon Press Inc
180 Varick Street
New York, NY 10014

Phaidon® is a registered
trademark of Phaidon
Press Limited

www.phaidon.com

A CIP Catalogue record for
this book is available from
the British Library.

ISBN 978 0 7148 6293 4

PHOTOGRAPHERS

Dennis Cox/Alamy
Schloss Stolzenfels, p100

Cornelius Paas/Image Broker/Alamy
Winterberg bobsleigh run, pp090-091

Iwan Baan
Jewish Community Centre, pp102-103

Holger Knauf
Cologne city view, inside front cover
Köln Turm, p010
Herkules Hochhaus, p011
Der Neue Zollhof, pp012-013
Kölner Dom, p014
Kranhauser, p015
Die Wohngemeinschaft, p017, pp018-019
Radisson Blu, p020, p021
The New Yorker, pp022-023
Hotel im Wasserturm, p024, p025
Savoy, pp026-027
Art'otel, p028, p029
Hotel Chelsea, pp030-031
Bastians, p033
Museum für Angewandte Kunst, pp034-035
Kolumba, p036, p037
Galerie Jablonka, Böhm Chapel, pp038-039
Lido, p040

K21, p041, pp042-043
Six Pack, p044
Kleines Schwarzes, p045
Die Kunstbar, pp046-047
Hallmackenreuther, p049
Elektra, pp050-051
Feynsinn Café, p052
Brauhaus Päffgen, p053
Salon Schmitz, pp054-055
Wein am Rhein, pp056-057
Le Moissonnier, pp060-061
Lena Terlutter, p063
Overstolzenhaus, p065
Schauspielhaus, pp066-067
Tonhalle, p068, p069
Wallraf-Richartz-Museum, pp070-071
Legal Illegal House, p072
WDR-Arkaden, p073
Gürzenich Ensemble, p076
Weltstadthaus, p077
Gerling-Areal, pp078-079
Utensil, p081
Jürgen Eifler, pp082-083
Herr von Eden, p084
Hernando Cortez Schokoladen, p085
19 West Furniture, pp086-087
Lanxess Arena, p089

Christopher Seelbach
Kölner Opernhaus, pp074-075

COLOGNE/DUSSELDORF
A COLOUR-CODED GUIDE TO THE HOT 'HOODS

EHRENFELD
Home to artists' studios, cool cafés and funky design stores, Ehrenfeld is on its way up

NEUSTADT NORD
A relaxed vibe rules here, as chain stores give way to local bars and independent cinemas

SÜDSTADT
This residential district has strong immigrant ties and boasts the verdant Volksgarten

KWARTIER LATÄNG
The university district is as knockabout as you'd imagine, although there are a few gems

DUSSELDORF
Just up the Rhine, Dusseldorf's historic core is not only well preserved but also full of bars

BELGISCHES VIERTEL
The Belgian Quarter buzzes with the city's choicest hangouts and best fashion boutiques

DEUTZ
The corporate giants and congress centres located here benefit from great river views

ALTSTADT
You could spend days exploring the Old Town, especially if you get distracted by the retail

For a full description of each neighbourhood, see the Introduction.
Featured venues are colour-coded, according to the district in which they are located.